UNMASK THE PREDATORS

THE BATTLE TO PROTECT YOUR CHILD

Home Security System
WORKBOOK

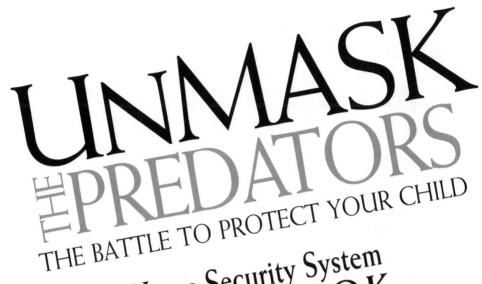

UNMASK
THE PREDATORS
THE BATTLE TO PROTECT YOUR CHILD

Home Security System
WORKBOOK

Lisa & Doug Cherry

HONOR NET
PUBLISHERS

Sapulpa, OK

Published by HonorNet Publishers

P.O. Box 910
Sapulpa, OK 74067
Web site: honornet.net

TABLE OF CONTENTS

YOU NEED A HOME SECURITY SYSTEM

Intruders. We spend time, energy, and money protecting our homes from invasion. Locks on windows and doors, alarm systems wired into the police station, motion detectors in our hallways, and neighborhood watch groups in our communities. But what alarms, locks, and strategies do we have in place to protect our most valuable resource, our children? Are we leaving them unprotected? Through *Unmask the Predators: Home Security System* we will help you, step by step, to keep your children safe from the dangerous predators hiding in the shadows. And they are most certainly there.

Perhaps you are like our family and feel your home is already protected from this threat. However, this false sense of security almost cost us our daughter and our family. Today in America one in four of our girls and one in six of our boys will be sexually abused by age eighteen. Stories about sexual predators hit the evening news on a daily basis. The homosexual movement has become the "new normal," living together before marriage has become nearly expected, and our kids are rejecting our biblical Christian faith in record numbers. Denial of these dangers is not protection. The ostrich approach by parents will never work.

Unmask the Predators takes us behind enemy lines to expose the enemy's work. The battle strategy outlined comes from the word of the Lord. But until we allow His voice to penetrate deeper into our parental hearts, until we tarry long enough to unmask the forces working in our minds, and until we grab His grace to change our behaviors, our children will not be protected, and we are in danger of losing our kids. And the baton of faith could be dropped. Permanently.

As we begin our journey together, I invite you to think of Doug and me as your personal coaches who will help you make the protective adjustments we all need. After all, none of us would intentionally put our children in harm's way. But all of us in this modern age must learn to disarm the predators before they strike. We will help you close the doors on danger, eliminate the vulnerable areas in your home, and raise a noticeable deterrent to hostile invaders who would seek to damage your child.

Sometimes we give room to the coaches in our lives—at least the ones whom we have voluntarily hired to do the tough job of shaping us. We let them say, *Lisa, you have now gained three pounds instead of losing one. You must have been sneaking more chocolate. Time to fess up!... Doug, you need to be more diligent in putting money into those investment accounts. Your future goals for your financial freedom are at stake.* And then we write a check for their help.

I don't know about you, but I could use a few more good coaches in my life, especially in the areas that are of the most importance to me. Raising our precious children to know the Lord and to serve Him would certainly qualify as vitally important, don't you agree? Hence the purpose of this workbook. We are after the "win" in this generation, so we are coaching the families of POTTS (Parents of Teens and Tweens) to dig deeper. Our generation is in crisis. Our homes are under attack, and the Lord is desperately trying to get our attention and come to our protection.

Doug's favorite coaching incident from his cross country days is the race when he made a wrong turn and then heard his coach screaming, "CHERRY! You idiot! Get back on track!" The race that day was on the line, and his championship status was determined by how quickly Doug responded to his coach and adjusted his action. In a similar way, the Lord did that very thing for us when we made a wrong turn in our home. And now we are testimonies of His power to help His children correct their course!

Coaching from man is good. Doug and I will do our best. But coaching from the Holy Spirit is priceless. Will you take a moment and ask Him to be your personal coach as we begin this adventure together?

The roles of the coach and the player on the earthly scene are set by design. Coaches are to stand on the sideline, observing, analyzing and calling the strategic plays. Players are the ones that play. But thank God we are not raising our precious children with these same earthly constraints. Our Heavenly Coach went to the cross to die for our errors and then rose again to take residence *inside* His players! Now He is cheering us on and whispering the secrets of the game to all who will listen, lay down their ways, and take up His ways.

I don't know about you, but I say . . . *Bring it on Jesus, bring it on!* (Even if I do have to face the chocolate problems in my life.)

A Note for Fathers from Doug

Dads, let's face it. In most cases it is the mothers who pick up books on parenting. They faithfully step up on behalf of our children to deal with difficult parenting issues. But as you hold this book, I encourage you to rise up to the high calling of being Dad. Our children so desperately need us to take our stands on their behalf. This culture is chewing up our children and spitting them out broken, confused, and hurting.

Maybe you are a single father. Maybe you are raising children in a blended family. Maybe your marriage is strong. Maybe it needs a miracle. In whatever state you find yourself, your children need your leadership and love like never before. We can do it! If we as dads will surrender to the high calling of fathering and put our trust in God for wisdom and direction, He will release His power and passion through us. Then we will be able to skillfully guide our children through the storms of this world into the special purpose and plan He has for each precious child we have been given. I can testify from my own fathering experience that seeing Kalyn and my other children come through the challenges and battles of their teen years and on into their twenties with a firm foundation, a clear vision for life, and a passion to know and serve Christ is worth all the effort of fathering. No one could say it better than John, the disciple of Christ: "I have no greater joy than this, to hear of my children walking in the truth" (3 John 4:1).

HOW TO USE THIS WORKBOOK

Individual Use

This workbook is designed to accompany the book *Unmask the Predators* and the video course by the same title. As you read a chapter in the *Unmask* book (and watch the corresponding video if you have it), complete your study by considering the comments and questions in this workbook. We encourage you to have your Bible handy as you study, looking up the references suggested and allowing the Lord to pull you deeper into His word. Please do not feel overwhelmed by the writing in the book. Some of us love to write extensively; others would prefer to ponder extensively and then write briefly. Make the book fit your style!

We wrote this workbook in a conversational style as if we had the privilege of sitting alongside you as we pondered these important concepts together. Think of it as a private conversation. But recognize the true other party to the conversation is the Holy Spirit. He is our real teacher and aid. Be honest in your answers. Your transparent responses will not surprise Him! But they will equip you to grow your parenting to a new level with Him.

Small Group Use

The *Unmask the Predators* program has three components available to the small group: the book *Unmask the Predators*, this workbook, and a video curriculum. A group can successfully study this topic using whichever tools they prefer. Participants in your small group will benefit tremendously by owning their own copy of *Unmask* and this workbook. Advance study on the assigned chapters before the group meetings will, of course, further the depth of the discussion. However, different group members will have various levels of commitment to the process, so leaders need to adapt expectations to the style of the group.

If you are using the video component, you may consider showing the video teaching segment first and then assigning the corresponding chapters in both the *Unmask* book and the workbook. Question and discussion points can be covered in whatever priority you feel is best for your group. Perhaps you cover some questions in your group time and send some home as homework.

What kind of small groups would benefit from this study? Any groups of two or more who are eager to *Unmask the Predators* and protect families. This could include couples, moms groups, Bible study groups, parenting support groups, Sunday school classes, neighborhood coffee clubs, or business place cell groups. The possibilities are limitless. We have divided the book into six sessions, but feel free to adapt the program to your group's needs.

Privacy among your group members is important. Obviously, personal information shared by your group should stay in your group. Some questions in the study may be too personal for some members to share aloud. Keep the group safe and comfortable without putting individuals on the spot for their answers.

If you encounter family problems which are complex and overwhelming, avoid bogging down in details and stories that will keep the group from progressing through the study. Refer the family in crisis to appropriate caregivers who can help. Keep your group discussion positive and uplifting. Raising children is hard work. But it is the most important job the Lord gives us! Ban a complaining, child-bashing attitude and maintain a heart of gratefulness. The Holy Spirit will be welcome where we allow His attitudes to be our attitudes!

Please note as you use this workbook that the corresponding page numbers in the *Unmask the Predators* book are placed in parentheses at the end of the discussion and question sections. Reading the section in the full text will facilitate a greater understanding of the points we are considering.

How to Schedule Your *Unmask* Study:

6-Session Guide for the Curriculum: Videos are 20-26 minutes. Choose discussion questions in the workbook as your time allows. Your study will work with either the workbook or the video combined with your *Unmask the Predators* book. But all three pieces working together is ideal. Go to Frontlinefamilies.org for help.

Curriculum Video Guide		
Session 1	Video 1: Unmasking Our Homes	Workbook: Intro, Chapters 1 and 2
Session 2	Video 2: Truth vs. Deception	Workbook: Chapters 3 and 4
Session 3	Video 3: My Parents' "No" Saved Me	Workbook: Chapters 5 and 6
Session 4	Video 4: Preparing for Battle	Workbook: Chapters 7 and 8
Session 5	Video 5: Recapturing the Teen Heart	Workbook: Chapters 9 and 10
Session 6	Video 6: Predator Protection 101	Workbook: Chapters 11 and 12

For a 12-session study, consider studying one chapter a week and rotating the video program if you have one. For longer studies, you would use all of the questions in your small group discussion time.

Let's get started with a word of prayer:

Father, this is a tough age to successfully raise children to be Christ followers. We need Your equipping and Your wisdom like never before. Lord, will You pull me behind enemy lines right now and help me Unmask the Predators who are poised to hurt my kids? And then, Lord, will You equip me with your wisdom and power to build a positive home that is safe, secure, and devoted to You? I give You permission to teach me new things. I yield my mind and will to You. I refuse to be afraid anymore but expect You, God, to be the strength of my life!

Speak to my fellow POTTS friends also, Lord. Open up our homes for Your glory that we may raise a generation passionately in love with You.

In Jesus's name, Amen.

WHY YOU NEED THIS WORKBOOK... EVEN WHEN YOU THINK YOU DON'T!

In America today an estimated 1 in 4 girls and 1 in 6 boys will be sexually abused by the age of 18.* A family's chance of encountering a sexual molester exceeds the risk of most diseases we inoculate our kids to prevent. That is horrifying" (p. 1).

> ❯ Do these statistics surprise you? Why or why not? Who have you personally known who has been touched by these kinds of problems?

_____

_____

_____

_____

I recently had the pleasure of talking with a mom of a thirteen-year-old girl. With tears in her eyes, she relayed an interaction she had with her daughter just the week before: *"Mom...would you still love me if I told you I am bisexual?"* the girl asked.

Her mother was horrified. The predator forces were at work in their home. The enemy was not really the other sweet little teenage girlfriend who had confused her child with their bisexual talk. The enemy was a dark force

---

* Eliot J. Briere, "Prevalence and Psychological Sequelae of Self-Reported Childhood Physical and Sexual Abuse in a General Population Sample of Men and Women," *Child Abuse and Neglect* 27 (2003), 1205–1222, www.johnbriere.com/CAN%20csa%20cpa.pdf. (Accessed January 27, 2012.)

1

much more powerful than a thirteen-year-old. The indoctrination of her public school "sexual orientation discovery class" coupled with media images portraying gay as a variation on normal had worked. But who ultimately was to blame for this mess?

☐   Read Ephesians 6:12.

> ❯ Do you see evidence of the spiritual battle and the dark spiritual force in that story of the girl above?

_____

_____

_____

_____

> ❯ How would this girl's problem be considered another form of a "predator encounter?"

_____

_____

_____

_____

Consider the following statement: "The predators have been given easy access to our kids. And we adults are behaving like crazily deceived people" (p. 2).

> ❯ How have predators been given access to our children?

_____

_____

_____

_____

> How do you respond to the concept that we as adults have been deceived to let this happen?

_____

_____

_____

_____

"As Christian parents we tell our kids that God has a plan for their lives. Perhaps it is time to tell them that the devil has a plan for their lives also" (p. 2)!

> Have you told your kids these two facts? Do they believe it?

_____

_____

_____

_____

"Sexual predators are not new. Their stories fill chapters of our Old Testament history books; their names were called harlot and adulterer in Proverbs; and their wicked spiritual origin was labeled the city of Babylon in the book of Revelation" (p. 3).

As we turn through the pages of our Bible, we see the problem in the stories.

> What force of sexual predators do you see in each of these scriptures?

- Gen. 19:3-5_____

_____

- Gen. 34:1-2_____

_____

- 2 Samuel 13:1-16 _____

  _____

- Proverbs 7:6-23 _____

  _____

- Proverbs 5:3-4 _____

  _____

- Rev. 2:20-21 _____

  _____

- Rev. 18:1-3 _____

  _____

If your kids catch you studying this book, let them know you are working on unmasking the devil's plans on their behalf! Let's review again the purpose of our study as we close this introductory chapter:

"By the end of this book, you will have revelation of three key spiritual concepts that will control our children's futures: deception, truth, and parental authority" (p. 3).

> What is the Lord already showing you about your need to grow in these spiritual concepts?

_____

_____

_____

_____

☐ Read this quote from page 3: "Allow the heavenly Father to pull you behind opposing lines and unveil the forces strategizing against your home."

☐ Spend some time now asking the Lord to *Unmask* the forces opposing your home.

DAD'S POINTS TO PONDER

⇨ *When a predator attacked my child, it was more deeply personal and painful than words can describe.*

⇨ *We thought we were alone, but predator attacks against children are happening everywhere.*

⇨ *We must expand our definition of a predator much wider than a strange man in a trench coat.*

⇨ *The real "predator" against our daughter was not a man, but the spiritual force behind the man.*

⇨ *Until we recognize the multiple types of predators that Satan uses to assault our children, we are hopeless to defend.*

⇨ *In this sex-saturated society, each one of our children is being stalked in one way or another.*

⇨ *Isaiah 59:19—"When the enemy shall come in like a flood, the Spirit of the Lord shall lift up a standard against him."*

Chapter 1

A PERFECT FAMILY

The title of our first chapter raises our first question: Is your family "perfect"?

> Is there any such thing as a perfect family? Why or why not?

_____

_____

_____

_____

> What are the characteristics of a perfect family in your eyes?

_____

_____

_____

_____

> How about in God's eyes?

_____

_____

_____

Kalyn reported on page 6: "A wave of both fear and excitement rushed through my body. Surely no one would ever know."

> Did you ever have a secret that brought a mixture of both fear and excitement?

_____

_____

_____

_____

> Think back to your own childhood and adolescence. Did you have any secrets that were confusing to you?

_____

_____

_____

_____

> What does Proverbs 9:13-18 tell us about this issue?

_____

_____

_____

_____

I remember the day when our world came crashing down, not unlike most other days in our busy world. On page 8 I wrote, "I was distracted that afternoon with my stack of suitcases."

Distraction. The truth is that every day has its own set of distractions. Do you feel like every day is busy and intense in your home? Sometimes when I am in the room with my kids, I check myself because I am not all there. Can you relate to this problem? If so, how?

Traumatic moments—opening acts—surprises. It seems we cannot, by nature, predict them. How then do we live prepared for handling the unexpected?

☐   Read Proverbs 12:18.

"In defense, we hurled our words like swords. I, even years later, don't like to remember what we uttered. *How could you do this to your father and me? Why, Kalyn, why? You have now destroyed our family's reputation. What else are you trying to hide from us? Are you taking drugs too? Maybe we should take you in for a drug test right now! What on earth are we going to tell our family? Kalyn, you surely know that this will destroy our church*'" (pp. 10-11).

❯ Why is it so dangerous to wield our words to our loved ones like a sword?

_____

_____

_____

_____

❯ How can we change those "piercing" habits? Read James 3:3-8.

_____

_____

_____

_____

Notice the "me-centered" pain in our parental words. She was single-handedly shattering our "perfect family" image right before our eyes. Did you note our selfish motives? How should we as parents have more appropriately responded?

"That shocking night we didn't understand that the strange relationship between our daughter and this man was really a case of criminal abuse. *A predator had entered our home*" (p. 10). I remember how it seemed to me that we were all being held hostage. In reality, the predator had been present with us for a long time. Isn't that an unnerving thought?

☐ Read Matthew 10:26.

> What can we learn from this scripture?

_____

_____

_____

_____

Soul-led parenting that allows our human mind and emotions to dominate is dangerous. **Spirit-led parenting** is what we as Christian parents need.

☐ Read Galatians 5:16-26.

SOUL-LED Parenting vs. Spirit-LED Parenting

> Characterize in your own words the difference between soul-led parenting and spirit-led parenting.

_____

_____

_____

_____

> Which are you aiming for? Why?

_____

_____

_____

_____

The craziness of our situation was overwhelming. Read again the tragic description: "Who was this child now living in our midst? Her face was hard, drawn, and pale. With the usual twinkle gone, her eyes were sad, cold, and lifeless. Our normally levelheaded, intelligent daughter was now angry, rebellious, defiant, and withdrawn; even after hours of discussion, she remained stubbornly convinced that her parents were crazy to have a problem with this unlawful secret relationship" (p. 12).

As Kalyn became a girl we could scarcely recognize, she viewed us as the enemies of her life. How painful and how crazy was that?

> Have you ever known someone who fought against the ones trying to help them?

_____

_____

_____

_____

> How did that look and feel to the caregivers?

_____

_____

_____

_____

> Have you ever resisted help yourself?

_____

_____

_____

_____

Jesus often faced this problem when He wanted to help others.

☐ Read Matthew 19:16-24.

> Jesus had the answer to this young man's need. Why do you think he rejected Jesus's help?

_____

_____

_____

_____

☐ Close this session in prayer asking the Father to equip you to stand in the fight for your kids.

DAD'S POINTS TO PONDER

⇨ *The fact that my daughter could have been this deceived shakes me to the core and has given me a "wake-up call."*

⇨ *Because deception continues to increase, our parenting must be scripture based and Spirit led.*

⇨ *We must uncover small secrets before they become giant nightmares.*

⇨ *A crisis often confronts us without advanced warning. We must be spiritually prepared and alert.*

⇨ *The first five minutes of a crisis will make a huge difference in the long-term result.*

⇨ *James 3:2—"For we all stumble in many ways. If anyone does not stumble in what he says, he is a perfect man, able to bridle the whole body as well."*

TRAPPED, TORN, ADDICTED, AND CONFUSED

Kalyn, when she wrote Chapter 2 at the age of eighteen, made an interesting observation of her family life:

"As a member of a pastor's family, I (Kalyn) found security in our tight-knit clan. Our brood was larger than average in love as well as in size, and for as long as I could remember, family was always the priority. From fun nights at home to summer vacations, we enjoyed being together and loved one another dearly. We had been through our share of troubling times and good times, but in the end, our family always stood strong" (p. 15).

> How would you characterize the baseline of your home?

> What will your children remember?

> What is their set point?

_____

_____

_____

_____

> Are there foundations needing to be strengthened right now? If so, what are they?

_____

_____

_____

_____

Kalyn wrote on p. 16: "My heart began beating rapidly, for I had recently grown very fearful of my father, the man I had once adored. After having been Daddy's dear *K-Baby* for so long, I had been pushing him away from my heart. I was terrified that he would find out my secret one day and discover the dishonesty in which I had been living for so long" (pp. 16-17).

> Is that "pushing away" that Kalyn described always visible to us as parents?

_____

_____

_____

_____

> Why and how does a child push a parent away when they are hiding a secret?

_____

_____

_____

_____

"Living this secret life had become the norm for me: putting on a good-girl front during the day and sneaking around during the night" (p. 17).

> Are double lives common even in the adult world?

_____

_____

_____

_____

☐ Read Luke 12:1-3.

> What do you think the Father's view is on double lives?

_____

_____

_____

_____

Kalyn certainly discovered the truth of Luke 12. Things in darkness will come to light.

> Have you experienced the truth of being "found out"?

_____

_____

_____

_____

One day recently in our family's devotion time, our teens began pouring out their concerns to us about their Christian friends.

"Mom, somebody needs to tell their parents what these kids are doing and saying in secret," my thirteen-year-old emotionally proclaimed. His words jarred me to the core. For I knew he was right. So many of our kids are living a double life and even thinking it is normal! Have you ever noticed how people will say the most outlandish things on Facebook Saturday night and then show up piously on Sunday morning? Hello! Are we really that confused?

> What is a double life anyway?

_____

_____

_____

_____

> Are you confident that what you are seeing in your kids' lives is what others—including your kids' friends—would report as the accurate view?

_____

_____

_____

_____

❯ Do we, as parents, sometimes only see what we want to see?

_____

_____

_____

_____

Perhaps we should ask the same questions of our own lives. It takes courage to *Unmask* our own lives and the lives of our children.

❯ How vital is our honesty?

_____

_____

_____

_____

❯ Are we the same person in front of the kids, the boss, the friends, and the pastor?

_____

_____

_____

_____

Kalyn summed up a common problem in adolescence when she said on page 17, "In my naivety, I never doubted his intentions; and by the time they were clear, I was already too entangled to walk away."

❯ How gullible and trusting are our children? Do they believe they are invincible?

_____

_____

_____

_____

Later in Chapter 11, I share some of the many warning signs we should have seen in our daughter's problem. But in her writing here she alludes to a big clue we missed:

"I tried desperately to make a good impression on them. I faithfully helped them set up their church equipment each week, and I was the first to jump to their aid in public or private" (p. 19). She wanted to impress because this man had her heart. Take an assessment of your kids right now. Who do they impress, defend, or imitate?

Reread carefully the last paragraph on page 19. Kalyn briefly described the long, slow grooming process that ensnared her heart. Recently, while cleaning out some drawers, I ran across some of the dialogue we retrieved out of our computer's memory after the story came to light. I was sickened again to read his words within their pages of conversation:

> *I'm smiling because your hair is cool...looks real soft and touchable.*
>
> *Gee girlie you're cute.*
>
> *Makes me want to run my fingers through it, cuz it's soooooo gorgeous!*
>
> *I'll be wanting to chase you around to look at your hair...I do that a little now, but don't tell everybody!*
>
> *I LIVE for your smile!!*
>
> *I'll be following you all over just to see your hair!!! Hehehe.*

Nauseating, isn't it? But what little teen girl isn't fascinated with her hair and eager for someone to notice it too? These early internet discussions were clearly out of line. But we did not read them, and Kalyn did not perceive them.

> Could you see your child being naively lured into a trap like this?

_____

_____

_____

_____

Recall the way Kalyn described the pressure against her mind during the peak of the struggle. Read again some of her statements below:

"I grew increasingly confused yet controlled by the very thing that deceived me. My perception had become warped and my judgment twisted. I could no longer think rationally or reason with common sense" (p. 22).

"All of my thoughts, decisions, and actions were based on this growing obsession" (p. 23).

"I lived in a fantasyland within my own mind" (p. 23).

Researchers of the adolescent brain warn us of the immature, irrational, and faulty reasoning skills that are common in teen decision making. We cannot count on them to "think like an adult."

> How does this increase their vulnerability to predators?

_____

_____

_____

_____

I must confess that even after talking with many victims and doing research on the subject of sexual abuse, I sometimes have trouble "getting it."

> ❯ Why wouldn't a victim just shout out for help? Why would they not want to be rescued from their pain?

_____

_____

_____

_____

"I learned to pretend as though I enjoyed the sexual exploration and desires communicated to me by this much older man. Terrified of losing his 'love,' I went along with all of his perverted ideas, even when they made me feel filthy, violated, and used.... Deep down I longed desperately for someone to detect it and pull me out of this sinking pit" (pp. 23-24).

Kalyn longed for parental help but wasn't able to express it! So why did she fight us so hard?

> ❯ Are you prepared to become your child's "enemy" for a season? Why or why not?

_____

_____

_____

_____

I was shocked to live through the raw reality of adolescent depression. I could easily recognize Kalyn's depression when she expressed it by hiding under the covers, but it was harder for me to diagnose the irrational thought patterns and explosive anger as depression.

> Are you acquainted with the symptom list of adolescent depression? Could you recognize depression in your child's life if it were to occur?

_____

_____

_____

☐ Go to frontlinefamilies.org and click on the *Unmask* link where we talk about the symptoms of depression.

Some of Kalyn's words are tough for me to read even now: "The only prayers I prayed during this time were prayers of fury, begging God to take my life" (p. 26).

Interesting. She was praying. Not exactly the kind of prayers we want our kids praying! But atheists do not talk to God. They wouldn't need to.

☐ Read Psalm 10.

> What if our children lived through only the first half of Psalm 10 for a season without experiencing the faith-filled hope of the second half of that chapter?

_____

_____

_____

_____

> Are we prepared to stand with them though their faith temporarily waivers?

_____

_____

_____

_____

❯ Can you stand by them in love while they wrestle with God?

_____

_____

_____

_____

Kalyn writes on page 28: "Throughout this time, I made several feeble suicide attempts, but these only made me feel emptier. I did find some relief in self-mutilation (cutting). Punishing myself felt good. I found that if my physical body was hurting, I could momentarily forget my emotional suffering. I made a regular practice of cutting my arms and legs, making sure that I suffered intense pain. I knew that I was only damaging myself further, but I didn't care" (p. 28).

Cutting is considered a major problem in the teen culture today. I personally was horrified by it. But did you know this problem is anything but new?

☐   Look up the following scriptures and describe what happens in these scenes:

- I Kings 18:26-28_____

_____

- Mark 5:1-8_____

_____

Cutting or self-mutilation is clearly an expression of the Kingdom of Darkness way of solving a problem! Experts say it can be just a passing teen fad in your child's road to maturity, or it may be a serious precursor to suicidal behaviors. It should never be ignored by a parent.

If your family is dealing with this issue, check out our resources for help at frontlinefamilies.org. Do not give up until your victory is sure!

The point to ponder at the end of Chapter 2 says, "Denial feels safer for a victim than dealing with the true source of pain."

> Why is this statement not just true for the victim but also those around the victim?

_____

_____

_____

_____

> How do we avoid the temptation for denial as parents?

_____

_____

_____

_____

DAD'S POINTS TO PONDER

⇨ *When the shaking came to Kalyn's life, the foundation of our entire family was tested.*

⇨ *Because the margin for error as parents continues to thin, we must not miss the warning signs.*

⇨ *Regular evaluation of family priorities is critical as only the families who build on God's Word will stand.*

⇨ *As I was discouraged and tempted to give up, I heard the Lord say, "You are not defeated; you are just in a battle!"*

⇨ *Even when we are rejected by a child, we must put aside the pain and not reject them.*

⇨ *Kalyn's desire to die was more than we could bear. Our only hope was in God.*

⇨ *Hebrews 12:28—"Therefore, since we receive a kingdom which cannot be shaken, let us show gratitude, by which we may offer to God an acceptable service with reverence and awe.*

Chapter 3

THE DARK NIGHT

Part of our spiritual preparation depends on our willingness to study our enemy's tactics and preplan our responses to his moves. In 2 Corinthians 2:11 (*The Message*), Paul states it this way: 'We don't want to unwittingly give Satan an opening for yet more mischief—we're not oblivious to his sly ways'" (p. 32)!

> In what areas of your life have you found preplanning to be important?

_____

_____

_____

- Your finances? _____

_____

- Your health?_____

_____

- Your household management?_____

_____

In this chapter our goal is to prepare our minds, hearts, and souls for any tough days of parenting that may come our way. As we look at the story of my experience with a "Dark Night of the Soul," our goal is to demystify the pain in advance of the pain! However, perhaps you are reading this book while you are already in the midst of a painful experience. If so, this chapter should help you find your way out of the darkness and back to the light.

All through the scriptures, God and Jesus are referred to as "light." The devil and his forces are portrayed as "dark."

> Why is it important for us to clearly differentiate those images?

_____

_____

_____

_____

If we do not teach our children correctly the nature of God, they could be deceived into believing God is involved in dark activities. (i.e. *But Mom, I really thought God was telling me to not tell you I was going to that party!*)

> How can we know that God is never the author of sin? (See scriptures discussed on pp. 32-33.)

_____

_____

_____

_____

Consider this quote from page 33: "However, the world as our kids know it is a much tougher, unsafe place than we knew even one generation ago."

> How do you compare the world of today with the world of your childhood?

_____

_____

_____

_____

> What are some of the significant changes?

_____

_____

_____

_____

☐ Review the statistics found on pages 33-34 on teenage problems.

> Do these statistics surprise you? Horrify you? Disturb you?

_____

_____

_____

_____

> What teens do you know personally who would be represented in those statistics?

_____

_____

_____

_____

"Understanding the source of the dark night is critical because when darkness tries to invade a home, many competing voices of explanation can be heard all around that can frighten and torment a person's mind" (p. 35).

> What kind of tormenting thoughts can you imagine (or maybe you have already experienced) would torment a parent if their child was under attack?

_____

_____

_____

_____

Nights are seasons that end.

> Have you ever been in a dark season of your life that felt like it would never end? If so, when?

_____

_____

_____

_____

The enemy would like us to give in to his destructive plans while we are in his orchestrated season of darkness.

> What scriptures would you cling to if you were ever hit with a dark attack that seemed to not let up quickly?

_____

_____

_____

_____

> How would a "dark night of the soul" experience tend to differ between a mother and a father?

_____

_____

_____

_____

> What kind of pressures could you imagine would be put on a marriage if a mother and a father were experiencing a dark night?

_____

_____

_____

_____

> What would happen if the parents were separated, divorced, or unmarried and went through a dark experience in parenting a child?

_____

_____

_____

_____

On page 37, we learned about the battle in our soul between our "thinker," our "feeler," and our "chooser."

> How have you personally experienced this inner conflict?

_____

_____

_____

_____

"The dark night of the soul can be thought of as a 'second labor in the life of a child'" (p. 38).

That is not necessarily a pleasant thought, is it? Not many of us delight in the concept of pain.

> Have you or other families that you have known experienced a second labor as they were raising their child? If so, what was it like?

_____

_____

_____

_____

> Are you willing to go through labor again on behalf of your child?

_____

_____

_____

> What frightens you most about the concept?

_____

_____

_____

_____

As I described in my personal encounter with the dark night, I became keenly aware that my emotions could no longer be trusted as accurate.

> Have you ever experienced your emotions as "trustworthy"?

_____

_____

_____

_____

> Recall a time when you made a parenting decision while in an emotional fog. Did it work out well?

_____

_____

_____

_____

Learning to look objectively and critically at our own emotions can assist us in managing the irrational feelings that try to lead us astray. Let's review the list I encountered in the dark night season:

The Vicious Cycle of Pain

Anger → Guilt

Guilt → Embarrassment

Embarrassment → Mourning

Mourning → Helplessnesss

Helplessnesss → Fear

Fear → Anger

> Can you recall a time when any or all of these emotions became irrational for you?

_____

_____

_____

_____

> How did you handle that experience?

_____

_____

_____

_____

> What did you learn from it?

_____

_____

_____

_____

> Do you desire to improve upon your responses?

_____

_____

_____

_____

On page 42 I admitted to a very irrational response—telling Doug that maybe he should find a new mother for the kids!

> Have you ever wanted to quit an assignment and run?

_____

_____

_____

_____

I remember my pain at that point, but I chuckle now at my primitive solution.

What if, under the pressure of a dark night, your spouse said something ridiculous? I am grateful Doug extended to me the grace to express my pain.

❯ Could you decide in advance of the dark night that you would give yourself and your spouse some room with emotions? Factoring in some failure to our loved ones' responses can protect our relationships.

_____

_____

_____

_____

❯ Are there some emotionally charged words that have been hurled in your home under the pressure of darkness that need to be retired from the air waves?

_____

_____

_____

_____

Now would be a great time to extend the grace and forgiveness to yourself and others.

❯ How about your kids? What if they say some words to you that penetrate your heart and sting? Can you forgive them in advance?

_____

_____

_____

_____

Once I had learned not to take every random emotion thrown around our house into my own heart, I found a calming effect from the Lord that immediately improved my parenting performance.

☐ Try saying this statement to yourself out loud: "_____ (insert your name here), this thing is not all about you. Quit taking everything so personally."

> Can you sense the potential power in that declaration?

_____

_____

_____

_____

In Joshua 1, God commanded Joshua over and over again to "fear not." Fear is a lousy motivator for leadership. It will cause all kinds of serious miscalculations. Let's look at the story of a father of a preteen who was in severe trouble.

☐ Read Luke 8:40-56.

> What was Jesus's commandment to this father in verse 50?

_____

_____

_____

_____

> How is that same commandment critical to our preparation for battle?

_____

_____

_____

_____

☐ Take a moment and memorize this phrase from Luke 8:50. *Fear not. Only believe.*

☐ Now insert your own name at the start of that phrase. Speak to your own soul to obey the Word of the Lord:

Lisa, fear not. Only believe.

DAD'S POINTS TO PONDER

⇨ *In the midst of unbearable pain, I found myself not only trying to save my daughter but also my wife.*

⇨ *If we do not give up, then out of the darkest parenting times will spring forth the greatest family victories.*

⇨ *If we are to win, we must be convinced in our deepest being that God is for us.*

⇨ *Lisa and I are learning more about God's grace for parents; when one of us is down and weak, the other is strong and encouraged.*

⇨ *Our children are worth the battle.*

⇨ *Galatians 6:9—"Let us not be weary in well doing: for in due season we shall reap, if we faint not."*

Chapter 4

THE TACTICS OF DECEPTION

We begin this chapter with an interesting quote from an ancient Chinese philosopher who said, "All warfare is based on deception."

> Have you ever heard that quote before?

_____

> How do you think that quote relates to a Christian's spiritual battle with the forces of darkness?

_____

_____

_____

_____

☐ Read the following scriptures. How do these passages help us understand the tactics of Satan's deception in our midst?

- 2 Corinthians 11:14 _____

_____

- 2 Corinthians 4:4 _____

_____

- 1 Peter 5:8 _____

_____

The enemy roams around like a roaring lion seeking whom he may devour.

> How do we see this tactic of conquest at work within the animal kingdom?

_____

_____

_____

> Have you seen this plan work in families where one person's attack caused other family members to fall also?

_____

_____

_____

_____

> How have you seen this happen amongst a group of teenagers?

_____

_____

_____

Sometimes people talk about "herd mentality."

> Do we see a certain form of herd mentality among peer groups of teens?

_____

_____

_____

_____

> Is deception contagious? If so, how?

_____

_____

_____

_____

> How should we as adults respond if we discover contagious deception at work in our kids' lives?

_____

_____

_____

_____

"Christian families are a challenge to the devil's kingdom by very definition" (p. 47).

> What do you think is meant by that statement?

_____

_____

_____

_____

> How is your family—not just the pastor's family or the missionary's family—a threat to the kingdom of darkness?

_____

_____

_____

_____

☐ Read Genesis 12:1-3 and Hebrews 7:9-10.

> When God looked at Abraham, he saw the potential fruitfulness of his descendants. He saw the seed before we ever could imagine the seed. When He looks at you, what potential does God see in your generational fruitfulness for His Kingdom?

_____

_____

_____

_____

> Why would it make sense that the enemy wants to cut off your spiritual heritage?

_____

_____

_____

_____

☐ Read John 10:10.

> Have you ever thought how much of a "trophy" the demise of a Christian family's fruitfulness would be to the one whose mission is to kill, steal, and destroy?

_____

_____

_____

_____

We as humans are often handicapped by our own perspectives. We see the challenges in our families as painful ordeals, while God sees them in the full scheme of the larger epic battle in the spirit realm.

> How easy is it for you to have tunnel vision and miss the bigger picture of your family's purpose?

_____

_____

_____

_____

> Look at page 48. What does the word _deceive_ mean?

_____

_____

_____

_____

> How would a deceived person know they had been tricked?

_____

_____

_____

_____

"Can you see how the sexual predator must be the ultimate tool of the master deceiver?" (p. 48) One of the purposes of this study is to prepare us to detect the enemy's activities in our midst.

> How does the sexual predator grooming process that we are learning about mimic the tactics the devil uses to lure people into other traps?

_____

_____

_____

_____

Consider the elements used in grooming, such as false trust, lies, secrecy, threats, denial, slow desensitization, flattery, false security, and fear.

> How are these elements present in the traps of the following sins?

- Adultery: _____

_____

_____

- Promiscuity: _____

  _____

  _____

- Homosexuality: _____

  _____

  _____

- Drugs: _____

  _____

  _____

- Alcohol: _____

  _____

  _____

The Nine Tactics of Deception (p. 49)

In this chapter we will prayerfully evaluate some of the common deceptions infiltrating our modern minds. Refer to pages 49-51 of *Unmask* to read the thought processes associated with each of the nine tactics.

☐   Ask the Lord to reveal to you how these thoughts have influenced your mind, your children's minds, and your spouse's or other family member's mind. Then take a moment and identify some of the potentially dangerous results of these deceptive thoughts.

Deception Tactic #1…Satan does not exist. (This one is very common in the "educated, modern world"! Have you heard it often?)

> How is this deception evidenced in:

- My Mind:

_____

_____

_____

- My Children's Minds:

_____

_____

_____

- My Spouse's or Family Member's Mind:

_____

_____

_____

> What are the potentially dangerous results of deception #1 to my family?

_____

_____

_____

_____

_____

Deception Tactic #2...Satan does exist, and he is all powerful. (This is the other ditch to #1. I have seen whole churches gripped by this one!)

> How is this deception evidenced in:

  ■ My Mind:

  _____

  _____

  _____

  ■ My Children's Minds:

  _____

  _____

  _____

  ■ My Spouse's or Family Member's Mind:

  _____

  _____

  _____

> What are the potentially dangerous results of deception #2 to my family?

  _____

  _____

  _____

  _____

  _____

Deception Tactic #3...I can handle this on my own. (Sounds like a good, All-American idea. But is it scriptural?)

> How is this deception evidenced in:

- My Mind:

_____

_____

_____

- My Children's Minds:

_____

_____

_____

- My Spouse's or Family Member's Mind:

_____

_____

_____

> What are the potentially dangerous results of deception #3 to my family?

_____

_____

_____

_____

_____

Deception Tactic #4 . . . I am helpless.

> How is this deception evidenced in:

- My Mind:

_____

_____

_____

- My Children's Minds:

_____

_____

_____

- My Spouse's or Family Member's Mind:

_____

_____

_____

> What are the potentially dangerous results of deception #4 to my family?

_____

_____

_____

_____

_____

Deception Tactic #5…Moral truth is relative to circumstances. (I think this is the biggest deception of our age! It is killing our homes and lives!)

> How is this deception evidenced in:

- My Mind:

_____

_____

_____

- My Children's Minds:

_____

_____

_____

- My Spouse's or Family Member's Mind:

_____

_____

_____

> What are the potentially dangerous results of deception #5 to my family?

_____

_____

_____

_____

_____

Deception Tactic #6...I would never be tricked. (Whew, this one is so dangerous!)

> How is this deception evidenced in:

- My Mind:

  _____

  _____

  _____

- My Children's Minds:

  _____

  _____

  _____

- My Spouse's or Family Member's Mind:

  _____

  _____

  _____

> What are the potentially dangerous results of deception #6 to my family?

  _____

  _____

  _____

  _____

  _____

Deception Tactic #7... Life is all about me. (My Facebook. My iPad. My friends. My life!)

> ❯ How is this deception evidenced in:

>> ▪ My Mind:

_____

_____

_____

>> ▪ My Children's Minds:

_____

_____

_____

>> ▪ My Spouse's or Family Member's Mind:

_____

_____

_____

> ❯ What are the potentially dangerous results of deception #7 to my family?

_____

_____

_____

_____

_____

Deception Tactic #8...God's Word is not always true for me. (It might have worked for Grandma or the pastor, but...)

> How is this deception evidenced in:

  ▪ My Mind:

  _____

  _____

  _____

  ▪ My Children's Minds:

  _____

  _____

  _____

  ▪ My Spouse's or Family Member's Mind:

  _____

  _____

  _____

> What are the potentially dangerous results of deception #8 to my family?

  _____

  _____

  _____

  _____

  _____

Deception Tactic #9 ... Everyone's doing it. (Have you noticed that everyone is always doing it? Even in my generation, I said this!)

> ❯ How is this deception evidenced in:

- ▪ My Mind:

  _____

  _____

  _____

- ▪ My Children's Minds:

  _____

  _____

  _____

- ▪ My Spouse's or Family Member's Mind:

  _____

  _____

  _____

> ❯ What are the potentially dangerous results of deception #9 to my family?

  _____

  _____

  _____

"Behind every attempt to deceive 'just one teenager' or even 'just one dad' is a master plan to destroy a whole family, weaken the body of Christ, inject confusion into the body of Christ, and shipwreck destinies. Why? Because this is not a symbolic war between good and evil; this is a real war waged one home at a time" (p. 53)!

☐ Read Ephesians 6:10-12.

> What does this scripture tell us about our war?

_____

_____

_____

_____

☐ Read again the statistics highlighted on pages 53 and 54 of *Unmask*.

> Does it shock you to realize our Christian children are a small minority among their peers? Why or why not?

_____

_____

_____

_____

> Is it easy for your kids to stand up for Jesus among their peers in your community?

_____

_____

_____

_____

> ❯ In what ways is it difficult for you to stand up for Jesus?

_____

_____

_____

_____

We send missionaries into countries with similarly low rates of authentic Christian witness.

> ❯ How should it affect our parenting decisions and actions to realize our children are "on the mission field" in their daily lives?

_____

_____

_____

_____

☐ Read Isaiah 37:30-32, Micah 7:18, and Romans 11:2-5. Note the word *remnant* in each passage. The word remnant is not used frequently in our culture.

The only time I remember seeing it used was to describe a small piece of fabric leftover at the end of a bolt in the fabric store. Usually the remnant was discounted because it was such a small piece. But as I have considered God's usage of the word, it appears to me He has a different idea. I now think of the word remnant as *a minority of people set apart for a particular purpose.*

> With those thoughts in mind, what do you think was meant by the word remnant in each of those passages?

- Isaiah 37:30-32 _____

  _____

  _____

- Micah 7:18 _____

  _____

  _____

- Romans 11:2-5 _____

  _____

  _____

> Is your family prepared to live as a remnant for Him in this difficult generation? How or how not?

_____

_____

_____

_____

☐ Read Matthew 5:13-16.

> ❯ What does this passage say to us in the midst of our cultural battle?

_____

_____

_____

_____

In this chapter we have evaluated our lives and our homes for deception. Now we are ready in Chapter 5 to allow the Lord to replace those deceptions with truth. However, as we conclude this chapter, may I lead you in a prayer? If you are married, I encourage you to pray along with your spouse. You may want to pray these or other similar words:

> *Father, as I look around me, I see evidence of deception's powerful grip. My heart, Lord, is to expose every false foundation in our home and rebuild our lives on the truth. We need Your Holy Spirit to lead us into all truth. I humble myself before You and ask You to forgive me for believing... (List individually before the Lord the deceptive thoughts you detected.)*

_____

_____

_____

> *I renounce those thoughts as works of darkness, and I ask You to be the Lord over my thinking and reasoning. Please take back the ground I gave over to the enemy.*
>
> *Lord, our children have been ensnared in this evil generation. I can tell them to change their thinking, but that is unlikely to work unless You expose and convict their hearts also. Please grant them true godly sorrow and repentance. Help us to teach and lead them more effectively. Protect us from Satan's deceptions and cause us to remain alert to his tactics and snares. In Jesus's name, Amen.*

DAD'S POINTS TO PONDER

⇨ *When the secret deception became exposed, it first looked too overwhelming to defeat.*

⇨ *If we will listen, God will show us which deception needs to be brought into the light right now.*

⇨ *Deception tolerated will bring more deception, but truth received will bring more truth.*

⇨ *As we boldly parent this generation, we are seeking to destroy deception, not the deceived.*

⇨ *Each time we courageously bring the truth into our homes, the presence of the Holy Spirit is increased.*

⇨ *John 8:32—"And you will know the truth and the truth will make you free."*

Chapter 5

THE STRATEGIES OF TRUTH

As we begin this chapter, we are going to read the familiar teaching of our Lord found in Matthew 7:24-28:

> "Therefore everyone who hears these words of mine and puts them into practice is like a wise man who built his house on the rock. The rain came down, the streams rose, and the winds blew and beat against that house; yet it did not fall, because it had its foundation on the rock. But everyone who hears these words of mine and does not put them into practice is like a foolish man who built his house on the sand. The rain came down, the streams rose, and the winds blew and beat against that house, and it fell with a great crash."

Maybe you grew up singing the popular Sunday school song about the wise man and the foolish man. Maybe you only looked at these verses poetically and "observed them" in your mind. If so, now is the time to interact with these verses and place them as a central revelation in your family.

> See if you can list at least three ways these verses are important to *your family:*

1. _____

   _____

   _____

2. _____

   _____

   _____

3. _____

_____

_____

Building our homes on truth is absolutely essential if we are to stand firm in difficult times.

☐ Turn in your book to pages 61 and 62. The long quote from Josh McDowell concerning postmodern philosophy is worth our deeper investigation.

❯ As you reread this quote, list in your own words the major beliefs of a post-modern worldview:

_____

_____

_____

_____

❯ What effect does it have on our parenting if our kids believe that truth is only true for them IF they choose to believe it?

_____

_____

_____

_____

The false (i.e. sandy) foundation of postmodernism is quite similar to the foundation revealed in Pilate's life as he encountered Jesus.

☐ Read John 18:38 and John 19:1-16.

> How are our children asking the same questions that Pilate asked?

_____

_____

_____

_____

"Can you see what we are up against in our homes? Only the power of the Word of God will penetrate the deception that undermines our cultural receptivity to the truth!" (p. 63)

> Does postmodernism explain why so many kids are ambivalent to Jesus? If so, how?

_____

_____

_____

_____

> Would Jesus be real to a postmodernist? Or would His "reality" be dependent on the postmodernist's acceptance of Him as real?

_____

_____

_____

_____

> How would our children respond to our rules and leadership if they are affected by postmodernism?

_____

_____

_____

_____

> What will you do to counter the force of postmodern humanistic beliefs in your family?

_____

_____

_____

_____

> The next question we need to ask ourselves is critical. Do we, as parents, have a *passion* for the truth? Why or why not?

_____

_____

_____

_____

If we are to drive the deceptions out of our families, we must use the power of God's Word. But before we can do that, we must be willing to ask ourselves a penetrating question.

> Is the Bible my personal final authority of truth? Or am I, like many in my children's generation, still struggling with issues of truth?

_____

_____

_____

_____

Believing the uncompromised reliability, authority, and integrity of God's Word is so important to your children's future that I encourage you to investigate and settle this issue in your own spiritual life. Perhaps seeking spiritual counsel would even be wise.

A question about this issue of truth became a central focus for our recent local POTTS meeting. We asked ourselves this:

> If my child was confronted with a scripture, would he/she view that scripture as authoritative in his/her life? Or would that scripture and its resulting application merely be an opinion he/she was free to take or leave?

_____

_____

_____

_____

> For example, if a question of the sin of homosexuality came up in your home, could you, as a parent, use 1 Corinthians 6:9 or Romans 1:24-27 as a way to settle your child's confusion?

_____

_____

_____

> Can you see the vital need to help our children with this issue of truth if we are to protect them in a world filled with predator forces?

Replacing Truth for the Deceptions

Now that we have wrestled with the concept of truth, it is time to *use* the TRUTH of the Word of God to tear down those strongholds of deception we detected in the last chapter of study.

☐   Go back to your notes for Chapter 4.

> Which of the nine tactics of deception did you detect were operating in your life or the lives of your family members?

☐   Now open your *Unmask* book to page 63.

Each deception has a theme verse that opposes it called the *strategies of truth*. In the space below, list the key verses needed to oppose the deceptions you are tearing down. Just looking at them in print is helpful. Copying them in your own handwriting and then committing them to memory will make those verses come alive in your own life. Use this space to help you with this project.

_____

_____

_____

_____

_____

_____

_____

_____

_____

_____

My Key Verses of Truth

☐   Copy them from pages 63-71 here as you match them to the deceptions
    attacking your home.

1. _____

_____

_____

2. _____

_____

_____

3. _____

_____

_____

4. _____

_____

_____

5. _____

_____

_____

6. _____

_____

_____

7. _____

_____

_____

8. _____

_____

_____

9. _____

_____

_____

> Ask the Lord to give you specific revelations of these verses' meanings for your family. Record those below:

_____

_____

_____

_____

_____

_____

> Which verses are you committing to memory right now? Mark them with a star.

_____

_____

_____

> How will you do this? How will you keep these truths before your eyes even after this study is completed?

_____

_____

_____

We are using the same strategy that Jesus used when he opposed His enemy in Luke 4.

☐   Read Luke 4:1-12.

Note how Jesus spoke the truth out loud. Go back to your key truth verses. Speak them aloud boldly! Tomorrow, say the verses again. In fact, find a way to sow these supernatural words into your heart and mind. Put them on your mirror or tack them on your dashboard. Make them your screensaver. Do something memorable as you replace the lies with the truth.

☐   Look at page 65 and 66.

> What do the words *dunamis* and *exousia* mean for your family?

_____

_____

_____

_____

> What is your greatest takeaway from this chapter that will assist you in leading your children toward truth?

_____

_____

_____

_____

DAD'S POINTS TO PONDER

⇨ *The deception that first quietly, then explosively, invaded our home brought with it terror and a sense of hopelessness.*

⇨ *Because Jesus Christ is the embodiment of truth (John 14:6), when we invite His presence into our home, deception is driven out.*

⇨ *We have been given the power to overcome the lie that says truth is relative rather than absolute.*

⇨ *The greatest gift we can give to our children is to establish the Word of God as the final authority in our homes.*

⇨ *John 17:17—"Your word is truth."*

Chapter 6

THE PARENT'S PLACE OF AUTHORITY

W hat was your gut honest feeling as you read the story of Kalyn as she encountered the kids in our front yard (pp. 78-80)?

> Have you ever encountered a similar showdown scene in your parenting?

_____

_____

_____

_____

> Have you ever seen one in your church or in the marketplace?

_____

_____

_____

_____

Those kinds of parenting moments, when the parent's credibility seems to be on public display, I find to be very embarrassing. I am always cringing when I witness the interactions, hoping somehow that the parent will come out of the messy encounter honored. Sadly, it doesn't often turn out in the parent's favor.

> Do you find it socially difficult to be the parent who says no?

_____

_____

_____

> Why does a parental no, especially to teenagers, seem so against the grain of our modern age?

_____

_____

_____

> How do you think passive parental leadership opens the door to disaster for children and teens?

_____

_____

_____

_____

Respond to the following statement: "In this postmodern philosophical environment, 'parental commands' by definition are reduced to 'parental suggestions.' When combined with the difficult pressures of broken homes, multiple parents, and blended-sibling groups, many are left in confusion wondering, 'Who's in charge of this family anyway'" (p. 83)?

_____

_____

_____

_____

❯ Who is in charge in your family?

_____

_____

_____

_____

On page 84 Lisa shares her testimony of her early adult life: "I had discounted all the Bible scriptures relating to the concept of 'headship' or 'authority' or that nasty 's' word—'submission.' After all, wasn't this twentieth-century America, the land of the free and the home of the equal?"

❯ Can you relate to Lisa's struggle? How or how not?

_____

_____

_____

_____

❯ Does the concept of someone telling you what to do make you bristle?

_____

_____

_____

_____

> How about your children? Do they bristle at the concept of authority?

_____

_____

_____

_____

"The issue of authority is paramount in rescuing a generation from disaster. Our households must pass successfully through God's school on this issue. His system is not some optional plan we can opt out of if it doesn't suit our fancy. It is *truth*, and truth does not change" (p. 85).

> Why would this statement be true?

_____

_____

_____

On page 86 we read the account of a woman who was challenged in protecting her son from a potential predator because she was unable to tell her son no.

> Does this story alarm you?

_____

_____

> Would you be able to protect your kids by saying no to their dangerous behaviors?

_____

_____

_____

_____

Every child is enrolled in God's "school of authority" at birth.

> What does that concept mean?

_____

_____

_____

_____

How have your children progressed in their learning of obedience? Use the following questions from page 87 to do a diagnostic check on you and your family.

> If you have younger children, can you give them a direction and be relatively sure they will obey that direction the first time without complaining or delaying?

_____

_____

_____

_____

> If you have teenagers, does your firm but loving "no" change their direction, or does your no seem like only a suggestion blowing in the wind?

_____

_____

_____

_____

❭ If you are a wife, are you submitted to your husband's leadership?

_____

_____

_____

_____

❭ If you are a husband, are you obeying God's Word completely and sacrificially loving your wife?

_____

_____

_____

_____

❭ How is your family doing in the school of obedience?

_____

_____

_____

_____

☐ Read Matthew 8:5-13.

❭ Why was the man in this passage commended by Jesus?

_____

_____

_____

> How is the issue of authority intertwined with the issue of faith in this passage?

_____

_____

_____

_____

> If we instantly received the Lord's Word as truth as the centurion did, what would the effect be on our own faith in God's promises?

_____

_____

_____

_____

> If you are struggling with rebellion in your home, it is tempting to believe it is too late to make any changes. According to the Bible, is that true?

_____

_____

_____

_____

Do you as the parent need to repent of rebellious attitudes and behaviors before you will be able to effectively lead your family? Be assured your repentance will open the door for their deliverance.

> Are you willing to do that now? If so, stop and pray!

_____

_____

_____

_____

> How can sexual abusers and predators misuse this concept of authority and damage our kids?

_____

_____

_____

_____

> What do you need to do to improve your leadership with your children using the concept of authority?

_____

_____

_____

_____

> Name some specific action steps for you and your family.

_____

_____

_____

_____

Are you connected with Frontline Families Ministries? Take a moment and subscribe to our blogs and newsletters so you can continue your education and training.

☐   Go to Frontlinefamilies.org and subscribe to our blogs and newsletter.

We also encourage you to subscribe to our POTTS monthly teachings.

☐   Click on the POTTS link at Frontlinefamilies.org to learn more.

We help parents apply these teachings in their daily lives as we stand and pray for parents in the midst of battle.

DAD'S POINTS TO PONDER

⇨ *When Kalyn's rebellion became full-blown, we had a deeper understanding of 1 Samuel 15:23, "Rebellion is as the sin of witchcraft."*

⇨ *When a child is in rebellion, they need love, but the rebel spirit needs driven out.*

⇨ *Like never before, we must lay aside fear and step into faith-filled parenting.*

⇨ *The powers of darkness have no option but to yield to the authority God has given us as parents.*

⇨ *With the wisdom of God, we can know how to parent with authority and tenderness at the same time.*

⇨ *Matthew 8:27—"Even the winds and the sea obey Him."*

Chapter 7

PREPARING FOR BATTLE—
BATTLE PLAN STEPS 1–5

We have already established in previous chapters the reality of our spiritual struggle for the next generation. Before we begin this chapter, take a moment and evaluate your readiness for Battle.

> If a serious crisis hit your home in the next twelve hours that threatened your children's health, safety, or spiritual life, rate your level of spiritual preparedness to respond:

1	2	3	4	5	6	7	8	9	10

Unprepared   Prepared

> Do you desire to improve your readiness for battle?

_____

_____

"Normal parenting will produce its share of normal skirmishes that test our parental offensive and defensive responses. Over the next three chapters we will learn twelve keys that equip us for the minor battles..." Think back on a minor (or major) battle you have fought in your home already.

> Are you pleased with your parental response to that challenge?

_____

_____

> Have you ever accidentally escalated a minor battle into a major one by poor parenting responses? If so, how?

_____

_____

_____

_____

The First Five Steps

Step 1: STOP, Drop, and Pray

> Do you have trouble s-l-o-w-i-n-g down when you are faced with a tough situation?

_____

_____

_____

_____

> Why does it feel so hard to hit the pause button and not give a quick answer to our kids?

_____

_____

_____

_____

☐ Practice some phrases you could use to allow yourself time to think and pray. (i.e. *Son, this is a tough problem. I need a few moments to reflect before we continue.*)

☐ Read Psalm 142:1-7.

Crying out loud to the Lord is good! It does, of course, require some privacy.

> Can you envision a prayer meeting with the Lord before a phone call to a friend? Why and how?

_____

_____

_____

☐ Read Proverbs 25:11.

> What are the "apples" and the "settings" as they relate to our parenting? How do we get them?

_____

_____

_____

_____

Step 2: CALM Yourself in the Lord

"A soul giving way is not a pretty sight. Emotions charge into overdrive and rational thinking goes by the wayside" (p. 97).

> What usually happens to you when your soul gives way?

_____

_____

_____

> Is soul-led parenting (see Galatians 5:16-26) very effective? Why or why not?

_____

_____

_____

_____

> How will you quiet your soul when under pressure?

_____

_____

_____

_____

☐ See page 93 for suggested scriptures to commit to memory. Using God's Word to restore our soul is wisdom.

Step 3: REFUSE Condemnation

> How would you define the word *condemnation*?

_____

_____

_____

_____

☐ Read 2 Corinthians 7:8-11.

> Paul refers to godly sorrow and worldly sorrow. What does worldly sorrow lead to? What does godly sorrow lead to?

_____

_____

_____

_____

> How have you experienced either form of sorrow?

_____

_____

_____

_____

☐ Read Romans 8:1-2.

> We can equate worldly sorrow with condemnation. What is the promise concerning the issue of condemnation?

_____

_____

_____

_____

❯ What is the condition we must meet to receive this promise?

_____

_____

_____

_____

❯ How do we reject condemning accusations of the enemy?

_____

_____

_____

_____

Step 4: WELCOME Conviction

❯ What does the word *conviction* mean (see p. 101)?

_____

_____

_____

_____

❯ How are the following concepts related to the concept of *conviction?*

- Brokenness_____

_____

- Truthfulness_____

_____

- Forgiveness_____

_____

☐ Read 1 Peter 5:5-11.

❯ Why is humility so incredibly important in our ability to resist the enemy?

_____

_____

_____

_____

❯ What is the three-step process we must follow for proper repentance? (see pp. 102-103)

1. _____

2. _____

3. _____

❯ Do you have any repentance work that the Lord is convicting you of right now?

_____

_____

_____

❯ Are there any sins standing between you and your children?

_____

_____

_____

❯ You and your spouse?

_____

_____

_____

❯ You and your God?

_____

_____

_____

Now is the time to take these matters to the Lord in prayer. Perhaps it is also appropriate to go to the one you have wronged and apologize.

❯ List any action steps you need to follow up with:

_____

_____

_____

_____

_____

Step 5: DECLARE Your Promises

"We get the power of God's Word working in our lives by asking the Lord to guide us to the scriptures specific for our situations and then personalizing them" (p. 107).

☐   If you have not done so, turn to Tool 1 found on pages 197-204.

Today, pray this scriptural prayer out loud in your own home or with your study group. Notice how each section is designed to strengthen you as a parent. Perhaps this whole prayer would be helpful for you to pray on a regular basis. I have personally found the Lord faithful to perform His word over our lives as I have faithfully prayed His word back to Him. What is your strategy for declaring the promises of God over your family?

The promises of God cover every area of our family's needs. List the specific needs you want to find a corresponding Bible promise to cover. You can use an online Bible study tool (such as Biblegateway.com) to help you find the needed scriptures.

_____

_____

_____

_____

_____

_____

_____

_____

Do not leave this step until you have your Bible and prayer strategy. Your family's readiness and protection are at stake!

DAD'S POINTS TO PONDER

⇨ *When "all hell" broke loose in our home, we would have been destroyed without a heavenly battle plan.*

⇨ *It is more difficult to develop your battle plan during a crisis than before.*

⇨ *As we refused to give in to the discouragement and to look to Christ, He showed us which battle strategy to use at every point throughout the crisis.*

⇨ *We must avoid the temptation to use worldly strategy to war against spiritual attacks.*

⇨ *If we avoid the temptation to turn against our spouse when our family is under siege, God will anoint both husband and wife with supernatural battle strategies.*

⇨ *2 Corinthians 10:4—"For the weapons of our warfare are not of the flesh, but divinely powerful."*

Chapter 8

BUILDING YOUR STRATEGY—
BATTLE PLAN STEP 6

In this chapter we will apply the principles of Building Your Strategy two different ways.

Step 6: RECEIVE Your Battle Strategy

First, we will learn how to be ready to receive a battle strategy that is specific to our family's needs, and secondly, we will examine the elements of the battle strategy the Lord gave us with Kalyn as a working example. I believe as we dig deeper into what the Lord taught us about her situation, you will be able to increase your awareness and alertness in your home.

How to be Ready to Receive a Battle Strategy

We can look into our Bibles to find examples of the Lord giving specific instructions to His children when they were in tough situations.

☐   Look up the scriptures below.

> ❯ How did each of these men and women receive their instruction?

   ▪ Noah: Genesis 6:13-22 _____

   _____

   ▪ Abraham: Genesis 22:1-14 _____

   _____

- Isaac: Genesis 26:1-6 _____

  _____

- Joseph: Genesis 37:5-11; 40:5-23; 41:15-36 _____

  _____

- Joshua: Joshua 6:1-20; 10:6-14 _____

  _____

- Naaman: 2 Kings 5:1-14 _____

  _____

- Jehoshaphat: 2 Chronicles 20:1-30 _____

  _____

- Peter: Luke 5:1-11 _____

  _____

- 120 men and women: Acts 1:12-14, 2:1-4 _____

  _____

› As you read these different accounts of the Lord's intervention, what did you notice are some of the common elements necessary for God's people to hear His voice?

_____

_____

_____

_____

> Are you prepared to employ those critical elements in your own life to receive a battle strategy from the Lord? Why or why not?

_____

_____

_____

_____

"You can be encouraged in the Lord that no matter what kind of battle you could face in your home, God has a plan for your victory. It will be unique and individual to your particular situation. It will be filled with wisdom and seasoned with His grace. And it will work" (p. 119)!

> Do you believe this statement?

_____

> Have you seen the Lord's activity in your own life before or in the lives of your family and friends?

_____

_____

_____

_____

> Are you ready to trust Him?

_____

_____

_____

_____

A Deeper Analysis of the Battle Plan the Lord Gave Us

I remember so many moments in our intense days of crisis when I would say half-hysterically and half-furiously, "Doug, WHAT are we going to do?!" As if he had any better ideas than I did! I hated the problem we were up against, but almost equally as bad in my mind was the uncertainty of not knowing what was going to happen next.

I still have trouble understanding how we could have been so confused about Kalyn's behavior in the early days. But I have to remind myself that I am looking back through a very different lens. I did not have the knowledge I needed at that time.

Going off alone with the Lord to seek His direction and understanding proved critical for us (see account on pp. 112-118.) I needed an education on some things, and He graciously directed my steps. The books I read were truly ordained from Him. God is able and eager to direct the paths of those who commit their works unto Him. I am very grateful for His leadership so that I could gain a heart of wisdom when I so desperately needed it!

Has God ever orchestrated your life in such a way that you read a book or saw a video or heard a friend talk "at just the right time" about "just the right thing"? Perhaps at the time you did not recognize His intervention. Perhaps you were even tempted to think it was just a "coincidence." Record some of those incidents here:

_____

_____

_____

_____

_____

_____

☐ Read Proverbs 3:5-6 and John 16:7-13.

› What do these scriptures tell us about the leadership of the Lord?

_____

_____

_____

_____

☐ Read the quote in the middle of page 114.

› Is it hard to believe how words and images could do so much damage in kids' lives? Why or why not?

_____

_____

_____

_____

› What implication does this information have for our kids who are bombarded with media?

_____

_____

_____

_____

I included a section of my journal writings on pages 205-208. The wisdom contained in that writing proved to be incredibly accurate. I found it amazing that when I was truly able to hear the voice of God for instruction, He was able to birth compassion inside of me for my daughter. Hearing His voice caused me to discover His heart for my little girl.

❯ Has the Lord ever led you in an instruction that proved to be vital?

_____

_____

_____

_____

When that happens, our respect for Him increases. He is absolute wisdom, absolute power, absolute leadership.

❯ Why would we ever settle for anything less than His best plan?

_____

_____

_____

_____

I loved the book *Rees Howells: Intercessor* by Norman Grubb. Through this remarkable life testimony, God altered my view of Kalyn and created in me an ability to see her as He saw her.

❯ Have you experienced Him changing your heart into a representation of His heart? If so, how?

_____

_____

_____

_____

> Do you need Him to do that now for you and your child?

_____

_____

_____

_____

> What would you do if you were desperate to hear the voice of the Lord for instruction and wisdom?

_____

_____

_____

☐ See James 1:5; John 16:13; Psalm 25:5; Psalm 37: 5-9; and Proverbs 3:5-6 for important Biblical keys.

> List those keys for wisdom below:

_____

_____

_____

_____

_____

_____

> ❯ What are your most important takeaways from this chapter to help you be ready to tap into the battle strategies of the Lord?

_____

_____

_____

_____

DAD'S POINTS TO PONDER

⇨ *When the tsunami sized crisis hit our family, I am grateful that Lisa, our son Nathan, and I had previously been taught to hear the voice of the Spirit.*

⇨ *When family strife hits your home, do not yield to the pressure to back off your pursuit of God.*

⇨ *It is not until you are committed to follow God's strategy that He will give you one.*

⇨ *God unfolded a divine strategy to King Jehoshaphat in 2 Chronicles 20 only after the King cried out to God, "We do not know what to do, but our eyes are on you."*

⇨ *Know this: God's perfect plan for your family's deliverance has already been written in heaven.*

⇨ *2 Chronicles 16:9—"For the eyes of the Lord move to and fro throughout the earth that He may strongly support those whose heart is completely His."*

Chapter 9

FIGHTING TO WIN—
BATTLE PLAN STEPS 7–12

I don't know about you, but I hate to lose! If I am going to have to battle at something, I want a winning strategy. Let's continue our preparation for WINNING by learning Step 7 of our plan.

Step 7: <u>FIGHT on Your Knees</u> and Act in Love

> What does the phrase "fight on your knees" mean to you personally?

_____

_____

_____

_____

> Have you ever waged a battle in prayer before?

_____

_____

_____

_____

> ❯ Most of us are familiar with prayers thrown up in desperation...the "HELP ME!" style...but do you feel equipped to pray through a season of battle? Why or why not?

_____

_____

_____

_____

"Sometimes during the intensity of our struggles, my own mind would scream, 'You don't know how to pray right anyway'" (p. 122).

> ❯ Why is it important to gain a heart of confidence in our ability to pray?

_____

_____

_____

_____

Consider the danger of entering into battle with the voice of the accuser screaming in your ear about your own inadequacy...and you falling victim to believing him!

Let's look at some important scriptures on the subject of prayer. Our goal is to settle in our own heart that we can pray effectively even if our own emotions are challenged because of life circumstances.

☐ Look up each scripture below. What clue does each one give us as to the value of prayer and the methodology of prayer?

- Jonah 2:1 _____

_____

- 1 Chronicles 5:18-20 _____

  _____

- Acts 16:22-28 _____

  _____

- Mark 11:22-25 _____

  _____

- Romans 8:26-27 _____

  _____

- 1 Thessalonians 5:17 _____

  _____

- Philippians 4:4-7 _____

  _____

- James 5:13-16 _____

  _____

☐   Take a few minutes and meditate on Luke 11:1-4 and Matthew 6:5-15.

Note how Jesus's disciples were expressing to Him the same question we are considering. *Help me, Lord. I don't know how you want me to pray.* We have made His answer into such a "religious reciting" that sometimes we miss the obvious. Jesus was solving their inner anxiety by providing them with a model.

☐   Now go back and say each phrase of the Lord's Prayer separately.

Did you know it can become your outline for a session of prayer in which you honestly communicate with your God? It might sound something like this:

Our Father which art in heaven… *Abba, Daddy, I love You. I thank You for being with me now hearing my prayers. Lord, even though I know You are in heaven in Your full glory, thank You that You are right here with me now, too. (This is your entry point to the Father. He is inviting you to call Him Daddy!)*

Hallowed be thy name… *Holy, Holy, Holy are You Lord. I lift up Your name, Jesus. I praise You and magnify You. You are the King of Kings, the Lord of Lords, the Great I Am. (You can list many other names you want to worship Him with. Jesus is the name above every problem coming your family's way. Philippians 2:10-11.)*

Your kingdom come, Lord. Your will be done on earth as it is written in heaven. *Father, You have a perfect will for my family, Lord. You know what each of my children need this very day. You know their callings and their futures. Lord, let Your will be done here on earth as You have willed it in heaven. We yield to Your will, God.*

Do you get the idea here? Make this prayer your family's friend. When your mind is challenged, you have a direction for prayer.

> How would you begin to pray the next phrases over your home?

- *Give us this day our daily bread.* _____

_____

_____

_____

- *Forgive us our trespasses… as we forgive those who trespass against us.*

_____

_____

_____

Another strategy is to look right into the Bible to find prayers that Paul offered up as intercession for his friends and churches. We know John wrote about the issue of praying according to the will of God with these words: *This is the confidence we have in approaching God: that if we ask anything according to his will, he hears us. And if we know he hears us—whatever we ask—we know that we have what we ask of him* (1 John 5:14-15). What better way to know we are praying in the will of God than to pray using His word!

Can you see the effectiveness of praying these prayers by inserting your child's or your family's name in each one? These prayers get down into the roots of life issues. If our kids really had spiritual passion, wisdom and holiness, wouldn't most of your family's problems be solved?

☐ Look up each of these passages. Mark them in your Bible. Practice praying each of them over your own life, your child's life or your whole household. Record here the central purpose of each prayer.

- Philippians 1:9-11 _____

  _____

  _____

- Ephesians 3:14-19 _____

  _____

  _____

- Colossians 1:9-14 _____

  _____

  _____

You can also take a passage like Psalm 91. Insert your name or your family's names, and use it to pray God's will. See also pages 197-204 for my scripture prayer. Try that here.

_____

_____

_____

_____

_____

_____

_____

_____

_____

_____

Obviously, we could study many days on this topic and only just scratch the surface. But here is the bottom line. If you do not have confidence in your prayer life in times of peace, you will not be equipped in times of war! Make this issue a priority in your spiritual life. And I promise you *will* be able to fight on your knees when the battle need arises.

Step 7: Fight on Your Knees and <u>ACT in Love</u>

The second half of Step 7 is to...ACT IN LOVE. Have you ever been near the struggle I described on pages 123-124 where I ran out of natural motherly love for my daughter? If not, can you imagine the pain of finding yourself in that place? What do you think this concept means: "You will see the power of my love operating through you" (p. 123).

Understanding the scriptural concept of love is critical. Review the elements of agape love as defined in 1 Corinthians 13:4-8.

> List those elements here:

_____

_____

_____

_____

> How would you as a parent allow the Lord to love your child through you?

_____

_____

_____

_____

Step 8: RECAPTURE Your Child's Heart

We consider this step so vital in the battle plan that we devoted a whole session to it alone in the video curriculum. Doug has a special anointing on this topic. So Doug...take it away!

Thanks, Lisa. I do have a passion to capture and hold my children's hearts. It is even stronger after suffering the pain of losing Kalyn's heart for a season. One of the most important keys in all of parenting is hidden in the last two verses of the Old Testament. Let's take a look:

Behold, I am going to send you Elijah the prophet before the coming of the great and terrible day of the Lord. And he will restore the heart of the fathers to the children and the hearts of the children to the fathers, lest I come and smite the land with a curse (Malachi 4:5-6).

We must take a moment and grasp this basic but profound truth: Someone will hold the hearts of our children.

> What does it mean to have the heart of a child?

_____

_____

_____

_____

> Who do your children look to, who do they listen to, who do they follow?

_____

_____

_____

_____

> Comment on this statement: "Whoever has their ear will have their heart, and whoever has their heart will have their destiny."

_____

_____

_____

_____

In America we are parenting a generation that is disconnected from their parents. Their hearts have been lost. As a result, we do not have the influence we need to train, protect, and correct them. In this state, we are unable to disciple them toward lives of fruitfulness in God's Kingdom. They are being discipled by the world.

When Kalyn's secret became known to us, the resulting rebellion, depression, and confusion were almost unbearable. But the greatest pain was the realization that I had lost her heart.

> Consider this: What would you do if you lost your child's heart?

_____

_____

_____

_____

I purposed in my heart that my #1 priority would be to go back after her heart and recapture it.

> How do you recapture the heart of a child?

_____

_____

_____

_____

Consider these steps to recapture your child's heart.

✔ *Turn* your heart to your child. This is the first step in the Malachi passage. Allow God to fill you with fresh love and passion for each child. Reconnect to his or her world.

✔ *Pour* out upon your child undeniable, unconditional love without compromising truth. I repeatedly expressed to Kalyn my unfailing love, even while her rebellion was like a stench in my nostrils. I had to remind myself I was not battling against Kalyn, but the spiritual powers that had deceived her. I began to write her love notes, take her out to lunch, and I slept outside her bedroom door praying for her healing. I even took her out of the state on a dad and daughter vacation.

✔ ***Humble*** yourself before your child and admit your own mistakes. This softens the conflict in the relationship, and humility opens the door for God to pour in His grace.

✔ ***Demonstrate*** to your children their value to you by making it clear the priority they have in your lives by your actions, not just your words.

✔ ***Pray*** that God would restore your heart to your children and their hearts to you.

✔ ***Believe by faith*** that God will do just what He said in Malachi: **I will turn the hearts…**

❯ What do you need to do right now to capture and hold the hearts of your children?

_____

_____

_____

_____

❯ Have you purposed in your heart to never permanently lose the heart of any of your kids?

_____

_____

❯ Are you determined to go back after your kids should their hearts stray?

_____

_____

_____

☐ Make that commitment afresh right now as a determining posture of warfare.

Because of the personality differences and individuality of each of our children, recapturing a child's heart would look different from child to child.

❯ How would you minister to the individual needs of each of your children?

_____

_____

_____

_____

❯ What would you believe to be the most effective way to reach into each of their hearts?

_____

_____

_____

_____

Recapturing a child's heart will require time, energy and priority.

❯ Are you willing to sacrifice each? Honestly, would you do it?

_____

_____

_____

_____

_____

☐   Take a few moments and talk to the Lord about this issue.

If you have failure in your life and need to confess your lack of priority, now is the time to get free!

Step 9: CELEBRATE all Victories

> Why do we, in our humanity, want battles to be instantly resolved? Is patience a challenge for you?

_____

_____

_____

_____

> Are all problems and challenges able to be instantly resolved? Why or why not?

_____

_____

_____

_____

Consider the word *discouragement*. Most of the time we think of it as sadness or mourning. But actually the word has a deeper meaning. Break the word into its parts: Dis—Courage. Since the prefix dis- means "not," the word denotes a non-courageous state.

☐   Read Joshua 1:6-9 and consider what the Lord says about the word *courage*.

> Is it important? Why?

_____

_____

Discouragement is a spiritual strategy of the enemy. That is why the Lord commands us to take courage from Him!

> With this in mind, why is it important that we celebrate all "pieces" of our victory as they come our way rather than just waiting until the war is over?

_____

_____

_____

_____

> How will you avoid the dangerous state of discouragement as a parent?

_____

_____

_____

_____

Step 10: Get Proper SUPPORT

Proper support during a family problem would potentially involve help from family, friends, church members, prayer partners, pastors, POTTS group members, or professionals such as doctors or counselors. Take a moment and identify who your best support team might be.

> Make a potential list of helpers here:

_____

_____

_____

_____

> If you ever needed the help of counselors or doctors, what would be your family's method of evaluating qualified help?

_____

_____

_____

_____

> Do you have Christian care in your area?

_____

> Would you be able or willing to go outside your community if the need arose?

_____

_____

_____

As we seek out our own proper support for quality parenting, it raises the question of how we support other parents in our sphere of influence.

> Who do you know right now who needs extra support for their home?

_____

_____

> What might the Lord have you do to assist them in their battle?

_____

_____

_____

_____

> ❭ Do you have a local POTTS (Parents of Teens and Tweens) in your community?

_____

> ❭ Would you be willing to start a local group or simply be a family subscriber in your own home?

_____

> ❭ Are you subscribed to all of our newsletters, monthly videos, resources and blogs that would strengthen you as you parent your children?

_____

☐ Find out more at Frontlinefamilies.org.

Step 11: Stay in Your Place of AUTHORITY

"As the battle rages over this generation, God is looking for parents who will continue to stand in their place even when times are tough. Many have been tricked by secular ideas and concepts into abdicating their authority" (p. 134).

> ❭ What do we need to do today to avoid being tricked into leaving our position of leadership?

_____

_____

_____

Compromise is tempting when we are in battle. Compromise sometimes feels like the place of relief.

> Have you been compromising some things in recent days in your home that you know are mistakes? If so, what?

_____

_____

_____

_____

☐ As you acknowledge those compromises to the Father, pray now and make a decision to take back your ground. As you pray, ask the Lord for wisdom.

> Record your impressions here.

_____

_____

_____

_____

"Remember, no one else can effectively take on your role. Only you are anointed by God to be Dad or Mom to your child" (p. 134).

> Are you under temptation now to abdicate your role? If so, in what ways?

_____

_____

_____

_____

> What adjustments do you need to make?

_____

_____

_____

_____

Step 12: WALK in Faith and Patience

☐   Read Hebrews 4:1-2 and 6:11-12.

Many of us have asked the Lord for blessings upon our children. We have made our requests known to Him (1 John 5:14-15), and we have stood upon His promises (2 Peter 1:4.)

> How is the formula of "faith plus patience" critical for us to realize the desired results in our kids' lives?

_____

_____

_____

_____

☐   Read Ephesians 6:13-14.

Patience is listed as part of the believer's spiritual armor.

> What does this scripture say about that?

_____

_____

_____

Battle Plan Conclusion

> As we come to the end of our study of the Battle Plan, do you feel more prepared to handle a parenting emergency?

_____

_____

_____

_____

> How would you rate yourself now?

| 1 | 2 | 3 | 4 | 5 | 6 | 7 | 8 | 9 | 10 |

Unprepared   Prepared

The poster on page 139 is designed to be clipped out and posted in your home as a reminder.

> Where will you post this information?

_____

_____

Make sure you have this plan handy for anytime you are facing challenges with your kids.

DAD'S POINTS TO PONDER

⇨ *When Kalyn's words and actions became utterly repulsive, God's grace showed up, empowering us to fight the darkness but love our daughter.*

⇨ *When we are able to receive grace and mercy in God's presence, we can then dispense them to our children.*

⇨ *After Kalyn came through the crisis, she said to me, "When I was in my dark time, I saw you come out of your prayer closet with tears streaming down your cheeks. I knew you had been with God, and it deeply impacted my life."*

⇨ *Until we recapture the heart of our child, other efforts will be rendered ineffective.*

⇨ *Gratefulness for every small victory is the seed for more.*

⇨ *No circumstance can remain unchanged when we release our faith in what God has already promised.*

⇨ *Mark 9:23—"All things are possible to him who believes."*

Chapter 10

MY ROAD HOME

When Kalyn shares her testimony, she is always quick to point her listeners to this part of her story! God has done a significant miracle to rescue her life from destruction.

As you read her story, did you notice the "teen side" parallel of the Twelve-Step Battle Plan? I love reading her side as a fulfillment of the prayers on our parental side. List here some of those elements you notice in her story.

☐ Refer to the plan on page 138.

> What resulted from Kalyn facing the truth of her situation that day at the Dairy Queen parking lot?

_____

_____

_____

_____

Roller coaster recovery was not the recovery I wanted as a parent! When she went backwards in her development, it challenged my faith. Kalyn said, "At the same time God was working, the enemy pulled me into erratic, bizarre behaviors to keep me from the destination God had for me" (p. 146).

Even in normal child development, strange behaviors can tempt us to "freak out," as Kalyn called it. With over twenty-eight years of on-the-job training, I am less likely to be overwhelmed when my child does something unexpected.

> ❯ How could it help us as parents to factor in a little more "unexpected" into our "expected" with our kids?

_____

_____

_____

_____

☐ Read Luke 15:11-24.

> ❯ How was that day on February 10 when Kalyn called Doug similar to that Bible story (pp. 146-147)?

_____

_____

_____

_____

I am amazed with the speed of Kalyn's recovery once she encountered her Lord on that day during the fasting retreat.

☐ Read James 4:7. That scripture lists two steps for the believer.

> ❯ What are those two steps?

_____

_____

_____

_____

> What is the promise for those who follow the two steps (i.e. what is the promised result)?

_____

_____

_____

_____

Submitting to the Lord involved Kalyn's submission to her parents.

☐ Stop right now and pray for that same revelation to come to your own children!

Our experience in court was grueling. In fact, about halfway through I began to question if Kalyn was going to suffer greater harm from the process. However, the chance to totally relive the experience and sort out the truth from the errors proved immensely valuable to her life. Sometimes the way out of pain means a temporary step back into pain.

> Is there a "going back through" problem in your own life or the lives of your children that you need the Lord's courage to face?

_____

_____

_____

> How will you do this?

_____

_____

_____

The foundation for Kalyn's life had been set long before a predator attacked her life. The word of God had been planted, and though she tried to run from Him, she did not succeed! Parents, this should give us great hope. Every word of the Lord and every promise from Him are true!

> ❯ What does that say about the priority of our planting God's word into our children's lives today?

_____

_____

_____

_____

No life is too damaged, no pain is too deep, no situation is too complex for our God. Kalyn is living proof of His healing hand.

> ❯ What complex situations do you have the faith to pray for right now?

_____

_____

_____

_____

DAD'S POINTS TO PONDER

⇨ *When the phone rang the morning of February 13, I witnessed one of the greatest miracles ever known to man!*

⇨ *Kalyn's story is living proof that a parent should never give up on God's miracle plan for their child.*

⇨ *Through divine guidance, we can direct our children to the place of complete healing.*

⇨ *God has already developed a "dream team" to work alongside of us to fulfill His plan for our children.*

⇨ *We saw rebellion, depression, eating disorders, running away, death wishes, cutting, and sexual acting out, but none could stand against the power of God through the Holy Spirit.*

⇨ *1 Corinthians 15:57—"But thanks be to God who gives us the victory through our Lord, Jesus Christ."*

Chapter 11

SEXUAL ABUSE 101

In the opening pages of this chapter, I answer the question that so many have asked me. *Lisa, did you not see some warning signs that would have indicated Kalyn was in trouble?*

> As you read the list of signs I missed, were you struck that these signs would have been caught and understood in your family?

_____

_____

_____

_____

Surely, the saying "hindsight is 20/20" is true. But who wants to wait for hindsight? I am believing our study will give you the ability to see into your family's current life with greater accuracy. This chapter tackled the terms and facts that I wish I had understood before a predator attacked our home. To help make these terms a part of your long-term memory, I invite you to review them here by filling in the answers to these summary questions.

☐ Use the text on pages 159-169 to find the solutions.

> What is the accurate definition of *sexual abuse* (p. 159)?

_____

_____

_____

Sexual abuse may be classified under two main categories.

> ❯ Name those two categories and describe some examples of each.

    1. _____

    _____

    _____

    _____

    2. _____

    _____

    _____

    _____

☐ Go back and put a star by any of the examples above that you consider your family to be at increased risk to encounter.

> ❯ List some of the new things you learned about the nature of sexual abuse victims (pp. 160-161).

    1. _____

    2. _____

    3. _____

    4. _____

    5. _____

    6. _____

    7. _____

Sexual abuse trauma has both short- and long-term consequences (see pp. 161 and 166).

☐ Go to our website, Frontlinefamilies.org. Click on the link for *Unmask* and find the resources on the symptoms and side effects of sexual abuse. You will find a few different lists. Familiarize yourself with those lists.

> ❯ Do you see any warning signs you need to act on now? List below some of the symptoms you need to remember.

_____

_____

_____

_____

_____

_____

_____

Sexual abuse can lead to many other complex problems in the child's or teen's life. As we discussed in the book, those difficult side effects are often the ones treated while the underlying abuse is left hidden.

☐ Take an inventory of the teens, children, and even the adults in your life. Of course, it is important not to jump to premature conclusions based on inadequate data, but are there people you know right now that you need to begin praying for?

> If so, list below and ask the Father for His healing and restoration. Pray that God might use your testimony of reading this resource to bridge towards their lives.

_____

_____

_____

_____

_____

_____

_____

_____

> Are there others you need to refer to this book?

_____

_____

_____

_____

The concept of "grooming" MUST be understood by the modern parent if we are to keep our children safe.

> After reading and studying this material, how would you now explain "grooming" to someone who had never heard of the term?

_____

_____

_____

_____

> What are the differences and similarities between a "pedophile" and a "sexual molester or offender"?

_____

_____

_____

_____

A five-year age difference between our child and another constitutes a power relationship that makes it difficult for them to say no. Knowing that fact should impact our protection of our children.

> What practical applications can you see in your own home?

_____

_____

_____

_____

"Over 90 percent of the time the abuser is known to the victim and/or the victim's family" (p. 164).

› What percentage of the time is the abuser a relative?

_____

› What percentage of the time is the abuser a friend or acquaintance?

_____

› Which family structures are at higher risk for the problem of predators?

_____

_____

› Is your family at higher risk?

_____

› How about the families your children hang the tightest with (p. 165)?

_____

_____

› Sexual assault is the legal term for what illegal behaviors (p. 165)?

_____

› What percent of victims will not tell about their abuse for at least a year (p. 165)?

_____

› What percent of victims will not tell about their abuse for at least five years (p. 165)?

_____

> Why do you think victims are so reluctant to tell?

_____

_____

_____

_____

> What role do shame, embarrassment, denial and fear play in the slow disclosure of abuse?

_____

_____

_____

_____

I remember feeling like such a failure as a parent that Kalyn had not told me about her problem. My sense of failure caused me to make even more parenting errors in our recovery time. I failed to realize "it was not about me." Perhaps one of the best things we can do right now is get over the fact that sometimes our children have multiple reasons why they do not talk to us.

> What do you need to do right now to position yourself to parent your child even if a secret shatters your world?

_____

_____

_____

_____

> ❯ What can we do to make it easier for our children to tell us hard things that they know we would rather not hear?

_____

_____

_____

_____

Reporting sexual predator activity is not an easy thing.

> ❯ What are the two systems that work on this issue in each state (p. 167)?

_____

_____

_____

_____

We will look at some of the difficulties with the issue of reporting in the next chapter. For right now, let's settle one major issue:

> ❯ Would you report sexual abuse if it happened to your child? Why or why not?

_____

_____

_____

_____

> How do you respond to the statistic found on page 167 that only about 3% of perpetrators ever do jail time?

_____

_____

_____

_____

> What if you witnessed symptoms or behaviors that you believe may be evidence of abuse in the life of another child?

_____

_____

_____

_____

> Would you intervene? If so, how?

_____

_____

_____

_____

> What if you were to suffer embarrassment, inconvenience, or anger from others if you told?

_____

_____

_____

> What would be your moral responsibility?

_____

_____

_____

_____

☐ Read Psalm 9:16, Proverbs 6:16-19, Micah 6:8, Psalm 82:3, Proverbs 21:3, and Isaiah 56:1.

> What does the Lord say about the issue of justice?

_____

_____

_____

_____

"Sexual abuse prevention is the responsibility of the adult, not the child" (p. 168). With this fact in mind, let's conclude our study with the personal application of the 26 Keys For Protecting Your Child in Chapter 12.

Chapter 12

TWENTY-SIX KEYS FOR PROTECTING YOUR CHILD FROM SEXUAL PREDATORS

This chapter as the practical conclusion to our study will only be effective in our families if we systematically *apply* the twenty-six keys to our present and future situations. Therefore, the purpose of this section is to help you make decisions and build your personal plan. As you refer to this chapter of *Unmask*, you will read the suggestions under each of the keys and then write your responses and action steps.

1. Understand Developmental Vulnerabilities

> Ask yourself this question on behalf of each of your children: "How could the enemy work his plan most effectively against _____ (your child's name) right now?

_____

_____

_____

_____

> How could he capitalize on his immaturities and weaknesses" (p. 172)?

_____

_____

_____

_____

2. Keep Your Mental Watch List

Remember, we watch everyone, but we are not suspicious of everyone.

> ❯ Are there any people you need to watch even more carefully right now?

_____

_____

_____

_____

3. Limit Unsupervised Contact

> ❯ How will you limit and monitor unsupervised interactions between your child and other adults or older teens?

_____

_____

_____

> ❯ What are your personal standards for maintaining your own behavior with children and teens?

_____

_____

_____

If we are expecting others to limit unsupervised activity and submit themselves to protective standards, we must be willing to do the same.

> Which of your activities could make you vulnerable to false accusation of wrongdoing?

_____

_____

_____

_____

> What will you do to provide accountability?

_____

_____

_____

_____

Remember, we can talk with kids and teens privately while still in a public room. We can help kids with rides IF we have someone else in the car. It takes creativity and forethought to practice accountability.

4. Teach Your Kids

☐ Make a list here of things you want to teach your kids about sexual predators. Reflect on some of the greatest things you have learned in the previous chapters.

Here are some ideas to consider:

- Kalyn's story.

- Joseph's story found in Genesis 39:6-23.

- The path of deception for a young man in Proverbs 7.

- Talk about the issue of love languages. How would an abuser speak your child's language?

- Go to Frontlinefamilies.org for helpful websites that assist us in training our children.

- Role-play situations with your children. Practice grooming-type communications and ask your child to fend them off.

5. Provide Early Sex Education

❯ What are your sex education plans and how will you implement them with your children?

_____

_____

_____

_____

6. Recognize the Fallacies of Early Maturity

❯ How accurate is your maturity assessment of your children?

_____

_____

_____

❯ Are they placed in vulnerable situations that demand adult reasoning?

_____

_____

_____

> What adjustments and protections do you need to make?

_____

_____

_____

_____

> How old do your children appear and/or act? How do others relate to them?

_____

_____

_____

_____

☐ Teach them to recognize their own limitations of maturity.

7. Involve Extended Family

> How do you need to inform or educate your extended family to help you in abuse prevention?

_____

_____

_____

_____

> How can you involve your extended family in your safety plan?

_____

_____

_____

_____

8. Hire Computer Accounting

☐ List all the computers, smartphones, cell phones, tablets, iPods, and other electronics owned by anyone in your family.

- _____

- _____

- _____

- _____

- _____

- _____

- _____

> Predators can disguise themselves online. Are you prepared to protect your children?

_____

_____

_____

_____

Most of us need updated help to keep ahead of the technology and the dangerous people. As the parent *you* are responsible for every one of those pieces of technology.

> What is your plan of accountability and supervision?

In our family we hired the help of an Internet accountability system called Covenant Eyes. Go to Frontlinefamilies.org for more information.

9. Set Sleepover Policies

> What are your family's rules and policies?

> If you are going to participate in sleepovers, how will you teach your children about the common vulnerabilities and dangers?

10. Train For Obedience

> ❯ Will your children respond well to your protective rules?

_____

_____

_____

_____

> ❯ If not, what help do you need to improve the obedience and honor in your home? (Frontlinefamilies.org and Frontlinemoms.com can be of help.)

_____

_____

_____

_____

11. Hold Your Child's Heart

Continual assessment of your child's heart is a critical part of our predator prevention.

☐　Go back to chapter 9 and check for any action steps you need to implement to recapture your child's heart.

12. Express Affection

> ❯ How will you appropriately express affection to each one of your children?

_____

_____

_____

> When will you do this?

_____

_____

_____

13. Maintain Humor

> Name some specific ways you can "lighten up" your home with humor and fun.

_____

_____

_____

_____

Practice in your mind using humor to diffuse some hot situations in your relationships. Humor cannot be manipulative or wimpy, but humor can prevent soul-led parenting errors. If you are in a small group, try out some of your ideas with the other parents.

14. Watch Church Safety

> What are the sexual abuse prevention policies in your church? If you do not know, ask those in leadership.

_____

_____

_____

_____

☐ Go to our website for more information and links to help you update your church plan. Consider whether you need to volunteer more time at your local church to make those safety policies realistic.

15. Install a Dating / Courtship Model

> How will your children find their future mates?

_____

_____

_____

_____

> What is your family's strategy for dating and courtship?

_____

_____

_____

_____

> If you need further investigation in order to make your plans, what will you do to investigate your options and make decisions that will honor God, honor your children, and produce healthy marriages?

_____

_____

_____

_____

☐ Go to Frontlinefamilies.org to find our resources on this topic.

16. Demonstrate Marital Excitement

> How will your children learn of the joy of marriage?

_____

_____

_____

_____

17. Allow Style Expression

> Have clothing decisions become a war topic in your home?

_____

> Do you need to develop modesty policies but find ways to encourage and respect style and individuality expression? How will you do this?

_____

_____

_____

_____

> How will you handle your next clothing shopping experience?

_____

_____

_____

_____

☐ If you are in conflict with your child, stop now and pray for a peaceful resolution to this potentially explosive issue.

18. Decode the Role Models

This protective key demands constant action. Practice your decoding skills today. Look at your child's world.

> ❯ Who is popular in the media? Who in the pop culture is speaking loudly into your child's world?

_____

_____

_____

_____

> ❯ What are the lead news stories in your local community and the world at large?

_____

_____

_____

_____

> ❯ How will you "go into" your child's world so you can decode these voices?

_____

_____

_____

_____

Don't forget the printed literature they read as well.

19. Watch the Friends

> List your children's friends here.

_____

_____

_____

_____

_____

> Who needs to be watched, and how?

_____

_____

_____

> Will you do this?

_____

20. Monitor the Cell Phones

> At what age will you give your child a cell phone?

_____

> How will you monitor the calls?

_____

_____

_____

❯ Who are they permitted to talk to and for how long?

_____

_____

_____

_____

❯ How will you be checking the texting conversations on your kids' phones?

_____

_____

_____

_____

❯ Have you told them they are provided complete privacy?

_____

_____

_____

_____

❯ Do you need to make some adjustments to your practices? If so, how will you handle this?

_____

_____

_____

_____

> Have you considered retiring all cell phones to their chargers in a public part of the house at a set time each evening?

_____

_____

_____

_____

21. Investigate, Investigate, Investigate

> How will you stay on top of your children's world this year?

_____

_____

_____

_____

> What kind of sacrifices will this take from your life as a parent?

_____

_____

_____

_____

22. Stay in the Word

❯ What is your personal plan for Bible reading, study, and meditation?

_____

_____

_____

_____

❯ Will your family attend church services together? How and when?

_____

_____

_____

_____

23. Maintain Spiritual Alertness

❯ How will you maintain a connection with the Holy Spirit so that you will hear His directions and warnings?

_____

_____

_____

_____

24. Pray

Specific and regular prayer for our children's safety is essential!

> How will you pray for your family?

_____

_____

_____

_____

If you haven't noticed, this is now the third time we have addressed prayer in this workbook.

> Are you elevating its priority in your home yet?

_____

_____

_____

_____

25. Research Your Legal Rights

> What is your state's age of consent for sex?

_____

> How is that enforced in your state?

_____

_____

_____

I recommend seeking counsel from a local spiritual leader to learn more about the social service agencies and counseling services in your area. Unfortunately, receiving assistance in the confusing cultural climate we are living in is not always easy. If you have a local POTTS group, consult with other parents to hear about their experiences.

☐ Go to Parentalrights.org for more information on this important issue.

26. Forgive Freely

☐ As you complete this study, read Matthew 6:14 and Matthew 18:21-35.

> ❯ How important is forgiveness to your family's spiritual and emotional health?

_____

_____

_____

_____

_____

_____

> ❯ Do you have some forgiveness work to do today toward yourself, God, or your family members?

_____

_____

_____

_____

_____

Now is a great time to start over with a clean slate as you enter afresh into the transforming and healing grace of God.

As we conclude our time together, I think we should close with this word from the Lord:

> "For though we live in the world, we do not wage war as the world does. The weapons we fight with are not the weapons of the world. On the contrary, they have divine power to demolish strongholds. We demolish arguments, and every pretension that sets itself up against the knowledge of God, and we take captive every thought to make it obedient to Christ" (2 Corinthians 10:3-5).

ABOUT THE AUTHORS

Doug and Lisa have a heart to see families pass the spiritual baton to the next generation and fulfill the calling of God that is on their lives. For this reason, they founded Frontline Family Ministries Inc. in 1998. Doug completed his master's degree at Oral Roberts University in 2000 and made a career expansion.

Together with all of their ten children and now son- and daughter-in-law (and their growing number of descendants), they lead the various Frontline Ministries, including Victory Dream Center (pioneered in 1998), REALITY Youth Center, POTTS (Parents of Teens and Tweens), and Frontline Families Resources. As a business man and CPA, Doug also founded Doug Cherry Financial Services, a financial planning and investment business out of Carbondale, Illinois.

Joyfully married for over thirty-one years, Doug and Lisa know what it is like to navigate a family through both smooth-sailing waters and troubled, dangerous storms. Their sensitivity, passion, and wisdom equip parents to launch strong Christ followers for the next generation. As they enjoy loud family dinner nights, toy-strewn messy living rooms, and traveling and speaking to churches, parents and teens, they have found their Frontline for Him.

CONTACT US!

We would love to hear from you! Contact Doug or Lisa at:

Frontline Family Ministries
PO Box 460
Carbondale, IL 62903

Lisa@frontlinefamilies.org
Doug@frontlinefamilies.org

800-213-9899 or 618-525-2025

FRONTLINEFAMILIES.ORG

FrontLine
Family Ministries

Growing spiritual and healthy families

- ✧ *Unmask the Predators* DVD curriculum for home or small group use
- ✧ Daily online tips for parents
- ✧ Resources for parents and teens
- ✧ Timely topics for families
- ✧ DVDs, books, CDs
- ✧ Lisa's blog for moms
- ✧ Doug's blog for dads
- ✧ Prayer support
- ✧ Parent coaching

To schedule Lisa, Kalyn, or Doug to speak for your church, parent organization, women's conference, or youth event, call **800.213.9899** or **618.525.2025** or e-mail us at **Lisa@Frontlinefamilies.org** or **Kalyn@Frontlinefamilies.org**.

POTTS
PARENTS OF TEENS AND TWEENS

Join the ranks of Christian parents standing shoulder to shoulder.

PARENTS OF TEENS AND TWEENS

Growing Spiritual and Healthy Families

We are a national organization with local groups in churches and communities supporting, strengthening, and equipping parents of the next generation of Christ followers.

- ⋄ Resources and training materials
- ⋄ Monthly video seminars for families and groups
- ⋄ Online and personal representatives for equipping local groups
- ⋄ Prayer support and encouragement for families
- ⋄ Daily tips for parents called *Bites*
- ⋄ Speakers for local churches, groups, conferences, or events
- ⋄ Regional Parenting Conferences in conjunction with Acquire the Fire in cities all across America. Check for a conference near you at **www.acquirethefire.com**.

To join us as a family, start a local group, or schedule a speaker for your event, go to **POTTSgroup.com** or follow the link on **Frontlinefamilies.org**. or call **800.213.9899** or **618.525.2025**.